Voicing and Comping for
Jazz Vibraphone

By Thomas L. Davis

Edited by Rick Mattingly

PLAYBACK+
Speed • Pitch • Balance • Loop

To access audio visit:
www.halleonard.com/mylibrary

2363-6046-1073-8561

ISBN 978-0-7935-8854-1

Visit Hal Leonard Online at
www.halleonard.com

Contact us:
Hal Leonard
7777 West Bluemound Road
Milwaukee, WI 53213
Email: info@halleonard.com

In Europe, contact:
Hal Leonard Europe Limited
42 Wigmore Street
Marylebone, London, W1U 2RN
Email: info@halleonardeurope.com

In Australia, contact:
Hal Leonard Australia Pty. Ltd.
4 Lentara Court
Cheltenham, Victoria, 3192 Australia
Email: info@halleonard.com.au

INTRODUCTION

The word "comping," when used in a traditional jazz context, is derived from the word "accompanying," and it implies the same musical activity. When a chord-producing instrumentalist (vibraphonist, guitarist, pianist) is comping in a jazz rhythm section, that player is providing a rhythmic, accompanimental chord progression over which a soloist is playing a harmonically compatible improvisation.

The guidelines, exercises and examples in this book are designed to assist beginning, intermediate and advanced vibists in conquering the problems encountered in comping. Since a vibist has only four mallets with which to perform, there are vastly different performance considerations than those of a pianist or guitarist.

This book deals with voicing selection, chord-member selection, use of extensions and alterations, as well as voice leading and inversion selection. While most of the guidelines, examples and exercises are standard practice in jazz usage, there will be situations in which these techniques are not applicable. In the performance and teaching of music, the use of the words "always" and "never" is best avoided. (The author always tries to never use those words!)

ABOUT THE AUTHOR

Thomas L. Davis is Emeritus Professor of Percussion at the University of Iowa. With degrees from Northwestern University in music education and percussion performance, he founded the Percussion Studies program at Iowa in 1958. He directed the University of Iowa Hawkeye Marching Band from 1967 to 1973, and he was Director of Jazz Studies from 1984 to 1993. Davis is a well-known percussion clinician, writer, composer, arranger and performer, especially on jazz vibes. Davis is a past member of the Board of Directors of the Percussive Arts Society, and he has been a member of ASCAP since 1968. He retired from the University of Iowa in 1996. He lives in Iowa City, Iowa, where he continues to compose works for percussion.

CONTENTS

4 Chapter 1: Chord Symbols

8 Chapter 2: Voicings

15 Chapter 3: Comping

18 Chapter 4: The II-V-I Progression

29 Chapter 5: Standard Chord Progressions

30 Ballad

32 Medium Swing

34 Fast Swing

36 Jazz Waltz

38 Bossa-Nova

40 Samba

Audio Tracks

1 Ballad with vibes

2 Ballad play-along

3 Medium Swing with vibes

4 Medium Swing play-along

5 Fast Swing with vibes

6 Fast Swing play-along

7 Jazz Waltz with vibes

8 Jazz Waltz play-along

9 Bossa-Nova with vibes

10 Bossa-Nova play-along

11 Samba with vibes

12 Samba play-along

CHORD SYMBOLS

Chord-symbol notation as used in jazz has become fairly well standardized. The examples that follow are the ones most frequently used by composers and arrangers, and thus most frequently encountered by performers. It is necessary to understand these symbols in order to spell chords and to properly analyze chord progressions.

1. A capitol letter indicates a Major triad.

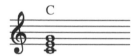

Pronounced: C or C Major

2. A small m indicates a flatted third. (Some composers use a minus sign, or hyphen, instead of an m.)

Pronounced: C minor

3. The number 7 indicates an added flatted seventh (relative to the root), resulting in a dominant seventh chord.

Pronounced: C seven

4. An m7 indicates a minor seventh chord. (Some composers use -7.)

Pronounced: C minor seven

5. A major seventh chord is indicated by maj7. (Some composers use M7 or a △.)

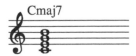

Pronounced: C major seven

6. The number 6 indicates an added sixth, relative to the root.

Pronounced: C six

7. The number 9 indicates an added ninth, relative to the root. (The seventh will also be included.)

Pronounced: C nine; C major nine

8 A 6/9 indicates an added sixth and ninth. (The seventh will NOT be included.)

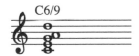

Pronounced: C six-nine

9. The number 11 indicates an added eleventh relative to the root. (The seventh and ninth will also be included.)

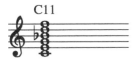

Pronounced: C eleven

10. The number 13 indicates an added thirteenth relative to the root. (The seventh, ninth and eleventh will also be included.)

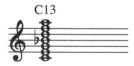

Pronounced: C thirteen

11. A flat can be added to the fifth, ninth and/or thirteenth.

Pronounced: C seven flat five

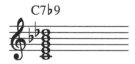

Pronounced: C seven flat nine

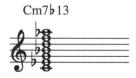

Pronounced: C minor seven flat thirteen

12. A sharp can be added to the fifth, ninth and/or eleventh

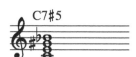

Pronounced: C seven sharp five

Pronounced: C seven sharp nine

Pronounced: C seven sharp eleven

13. A diminished chord is indicated by dim. (Some composers use the symbol ○ instead of dim.)

Pronounced: C diminished; C diminished seven

14. A plus sign is used to indicate an augmented chord.

Pronounced: C augmented, C augmented seven

15. The word "sus" indicates a chord in which the third is replaced by a suspended fourth.

Pronounced: C seven suspended fourth

Remember that, in this system of chord symbols, the word minor always refers to the third and the word major always refers to the seventh.

VOICINGS

Voicing Selection

Open Voicing refers to an arrangement of notes in which the distance between the outer voices of a chord is larger than an octave.

Generally, open voicing will sound fuller than close voicing, as it encompasses a larger portion of the keyboard. Because the intervals between the mallets in each hand are typically fourths, fifths or tritones, open-position chords are physically easy to execute on the vibraphone.

Close Voicing refers to an arrangement of notes in which the distance between the outer voices of a chord is less than an octave.

Generally, close voicing sounds rather thin, as it encompasses a rather small portion of the keyboard. Because the intervals between the mallets in each hand are generally seconds and thirds, close-position chords are physically more difficult to execute on the vibraphone than open-position chords, especially in the upper registers in which the bars are not as wide.

Combination Voicing refers to a situation in which open and close versions of the same chord are played in sequence.

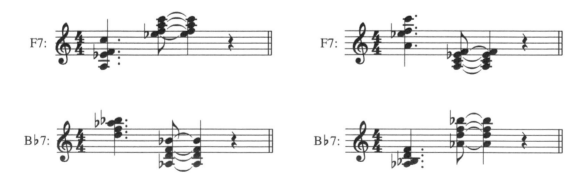

Combination voicings should be used sparingly, as they require the pedal to be depressed for several beats and can thus cause a cluttered sound. This can be remedied by releasing the pedal between each attack of the chord.

Chord Member Selection

The unique sounds of traditional jazz harmony are primarily created by using extensions of chords beyond the seventh scale degree. Following are some guidelines that will enable the vibist to create those sounds.

- The most important member of any chord is the third, as it identifies the chord as being major or minor.

- The second most important member of a chord is the seventh. The relationship between the third and the seventh identifies the chord as being stationary or being one that must be resolved.

As a general rule, then, always include the third and the seventh of a chord when comping.

Exceptions:

- On 6/9 chords (e.g., C6/9, Dm6/9, etc.), the sixth scale degree replaces the seventh, but the third is still included.

- On suspended fourth chords (e.g., G7sus, etc.), the fourth scale degree will replace the third, but the seventh is still included.

Extensions and Alterations

In a major tonality, on major seventh chords and minor seventh chords, replace the root of the chord with the ninth. (In a comping situation, it is generally unnecessary for the vibist to play the root, as the root is being supplied by the bassist.)

Open voicing

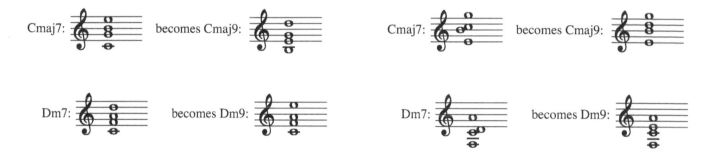

Close voicing

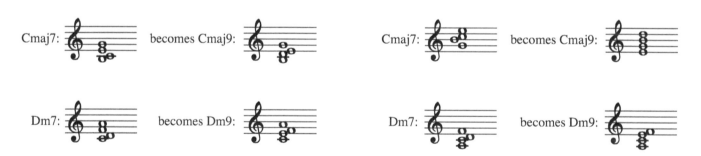

In a major tonality, on dominant seventh chords, replace the root of the chord with the ninth, and replace the fifth of the chord with the thirteenth.

Open voicing

Close voicing

10

In a minor tonality, on minor sixth chords, replace the root of the chord with the ninth, and replace the sixth of the chord with the major seventh.

Open voicing

Close voicing

In a minor tonality, on dominant seventh chords, replace the root of the chord with a flatted ninth, and replace the fifth of the chord with a flatted thirteenth.

Open voicing

Close voicing

An altered chord is one in which one of its notes is raised or lowered, or one that contains a pitch that is not a member of the chord or its normal extensions. When playing such chords, include the altered voice among the selected chord members.

Open voicing

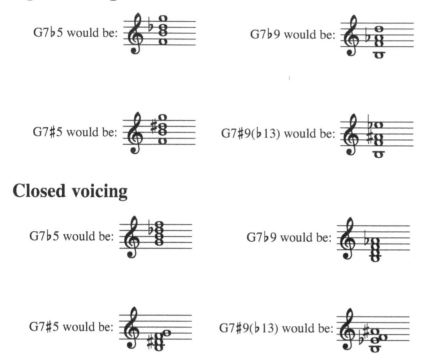

G7♭5 would be:

G7♭9 would be:

G7♯5 would be:

G7♯9(♭13) would be:

Closed voicing

G7♭5 would be:

G7♭9 would be:

G7♯5 would be:

G7♯9(♭13) would be:

Diminished seventh chords, whether in a major or minor tonality, are not generally extended or altered. It is not unusual, however, to encounter a melody note in a composition that is not a member of the diminished seventh chord over which it is played.

Examples of Diminished Seventh Chords in Open Position:

Bdim7:

Bdim7: with alteration:

Examples of Diminished Seventh Chords in Close Position:

Bdim7:

Bdim7 with alteration:

Inversion Selection and Voice Leading

In open voicing, try to play both the third and seventh with the left hand. This usually results in smooth voice leading.

In close voicing, try to play either the third or seventh in the lowest voice. This will usually result in smooth voice leading.

When a chord progression moves according to the Circle of Fifths (e.g., III, IV, VI, I, etc.), the seventh of one chord should, if possible, resolve down to the third of the next chord, or the third of one chord should resolve downward to the seventh of the next chord.

Open voicing:

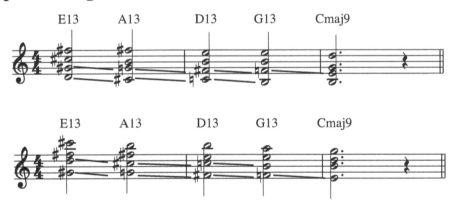

Close voicing:

Summary of inversion selection and use of extensions

1. In open position, try to use the third and seventh in the left hand.

2. In close position, try to use either the third or seventh in the lowest voice.

3. In a major tonality:
    a. On major seventh chords and minor seventh chords, replace the root with the ninth.
    b. On dominant seventh chords, replace the root with the ninth, and replace the fifth with the thirteenth.

4. In a minor tonality:
    a. On major sixth chords, replace the root with the ninth, and replace the sixth with the major seventh.
    b. On dominant seventh chords, replace the root with the flatted ninth and replace the fifth with the flatted thirteenth.

Note: It is important to remember that these are only guidelines. There will occasionally be instances where these suggestions are not desirable. Common sense and careful listening should dictate usage.

CHAPTER 3

COMPING

When comping on vibes, one does not necessarily have to use all four mallets simultaneously for every chord symbol. Executing the following phrase as written would sound cluttered, "ringy," rhythmically boring and much too predictable.

There are numerous ways in which to interpret a chord symbol and literally hundreds of rhythmic variations one can use. Following are eleven interpretations of a Dm9 chord, using open voicings and sample rhythms.

Note: The mallets are numbered in the following manner:

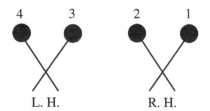

1. Block chord

2. Ascending arpeggio

3. Descending arpeggio

4.   Right hand followed by left hand

5.   Left hand followed by right hand

6.   Inside voices followed by outside voices

7.   Outside voices followed by inside voices

8.   Upper voices in each hand followed by lower voices

9.   Lower voices in each hand followed by upper voices

10. Upper/lower staggered voices

11. Lower/upper staggered voices

Due to the small distances between voices, close-position chords are generally played either as block attacks, by Right-Left attacks, or by Left-Right attacks (see examples 1, 4 and 5).

Consecutive block attacks should be rhythmic and staccato, not sustained. Use a short pedal application.

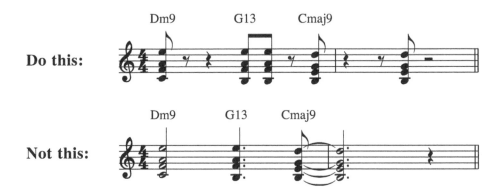

Use the ear to determine the correct use of the pedal. Inexperienced vibists often use too much pedal, which results in a cluttered, "ringy" sound. Three good rules to keep in mind are:

1. Use short pedal depressions.
2. Pedal whenever the harmony changes.
3. Mallet-damp whenever necessary.

When a IIm7 chord is followed by a V7 chord, one often docs not have to play two block attacks in succession. Rather, mallet-damp the seventh of the IIm7 while striking the third of the V7, while sustaining the other voices with the pedal. For example:

The above technique can be practiced with the chord progressions found in Chapter 4.

Register Selection

When comping, try to stay out of the soloist's register. Three rules to remember are:

1. If the soloist is high, comp in the low register.
2. If the soloist is low, comp in the high register.
3. Change registers as the soloist changes from low to middle to high, etc.

If you accidently land in the same register as the soloist, comp in extremely short note values and move to a different register as quickly as is musically practical.

CHAPTER 4

THE II-V-I PROGRESSION

The following pages contain examples of the II-V-I progression with standard jazz alterations in all major and minor keys. Each example contains an "A" voicing in which the third of the chord is in the lowest voice, and a "B" voicing in which the seventh is in the lowest voice. Both open and close voicings are shown.

MAJOR TONALITIES

Tonal Center: C Major

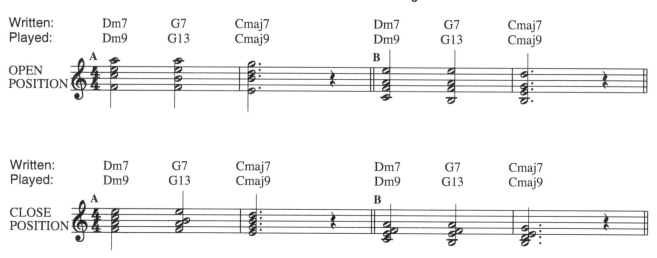

Tonal Center: F Major

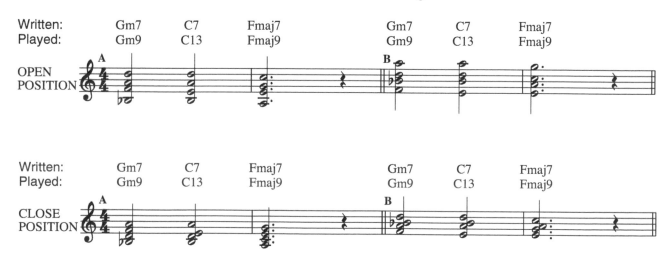

Tonal Center: G Major

Tonal Center: B♭ Major

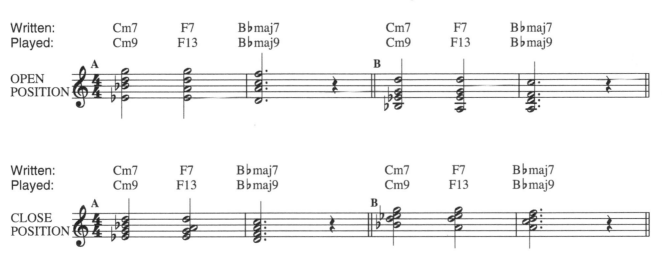

Tonal Center: D Major

Tonal Center: E♭ Major

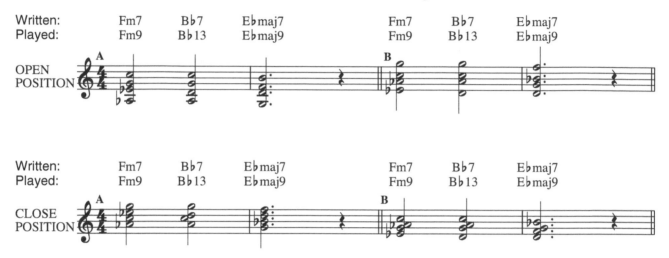

Tonal Center: A Major

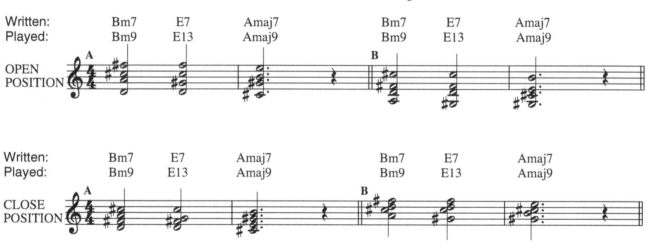

Tonal Center: A♭ Major

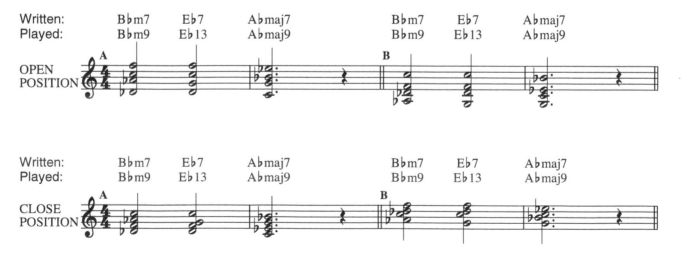

Tonal Center: E Major

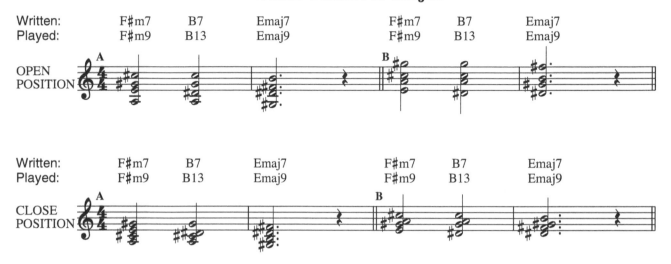

Tonal Center: D♭ Major

Tonal Center: B Major

21

Tonal Center: G♭ Major

Tonal Center: F♯ Major

Tonal Center: C♭ Major

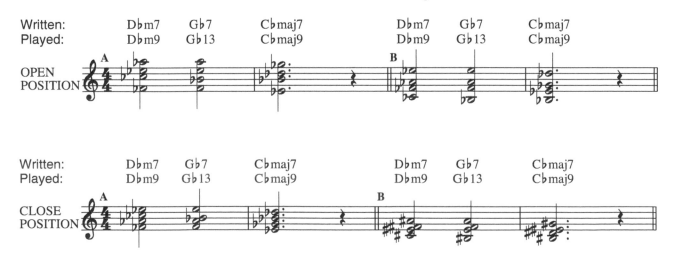

Tonal Center: C♯ Major

Suggested Practice Variations

In the preceding II-V-I examples, replace the dominant thirteenth chord with the following altered dominant chords:

1. V9♭5: use the 3rd, 7th, 9th and flatted 5th (e.g., for G9♭5, play B, F, A, D-flat).

2. V9♯5: use the 3rd, 7th, 9th and sharp 5th (e.g., for G9♯5 play B, F, A, D-sharp).

3. V7♯11: use the 3rd, 7th, 9th and sharp 11th (e.g., for G7♯11 play B, F, A, C-sharp).

4. V13♭9: use the 3rd, 7th, flat 9th and 13th (e.g., for G13♭9 play B, F, A-flat, E).

5. V7♯9(♭13): Use the 3rd, 7th, sharp 9th and flat 13th (e.g., for G7♯9(♭13) play B, F, A-sharp, E-flat).

MINOR TONALITIES

Tonal Center: A Minor

Written: Bm7♭5   E7♭9   Am6   Bm7♭5   E7♭9   Am6
Played: Bm7♭5   E7♭9(♭13)   Am(maj9)   Bm7♭5   E7♭9(♭13)   Am(maj9)

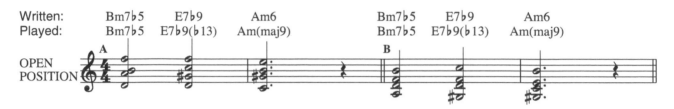

Written: Bm7♭5   E7♭9   Am6   Bm7♭5   E7♭9   Am6
Played: Bm7♭5   E7♭9(♭13)   Am(maj9)   Bm7♭5   E7♭9(♭13)   Am(maj9)

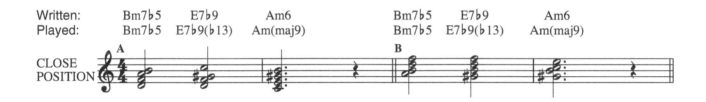

Tonal Center: D Minor

Written: Em7♭5   A7♭9   Dm6   Em7♭5   A7♭9   Dm6
Played: Em7♭5   A7♭9(♭13)   Dm(maj9)   Em7♭5   A7♭9(♭13)   Dm(maj9)

Written: Em7♭5   A7♭9   Dm6   Em7♭5   A7♭9   Dm6
Played: Em7♭5   A7♭9(♭13)   Dm(maj9)   Em7♭5   A7♭9(♭13)   Dm(maj9)

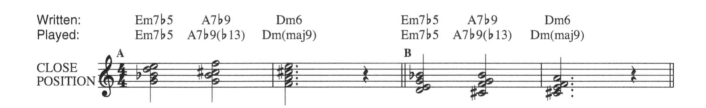

Tonal Center: E Minor

Written: F#m7♭5   B7♭9   Em6   F#m7♭5   B7♭9   Em6
Played: F#m7♭5   B7♭9(♭13)   Em(maj9)   F#m7♭5   B7♭9(♭13)   Em(maj9)

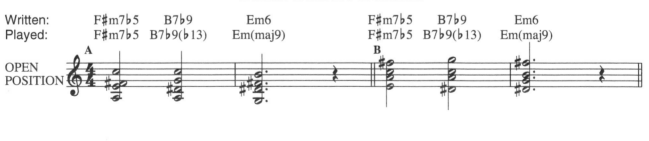

Written: F#m7♭5   B7♭9   Em6   F#m7♭5   B7♭9   Em6
Played: F#m7♭5   B7♭9(♭13)   Em(maj9)   F#m7♭5   B7♭9(♭13)   Em(maj9)

Tonal Center: G Minor

Written: Am7♭5   D7♭9   Gm6   Am7♭5   D7♭9   Gm6
Played: Am7♭5   D7♭9(♭13)   Gm(maj9)   Am7♭5   D7♭9(♭13)   Gm(maj9)

OPEN POSITION

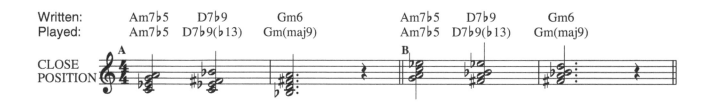

Written: Am7♭5   D7♭9   Gm6   Am7♭5   D7♭9   Gm6
Played: Am7♭5   D7♭9(♭13)   Gm(maj9)   Am7♭5   D7♭9(♭13)   Gm(maj9)

CLOSE POSITION

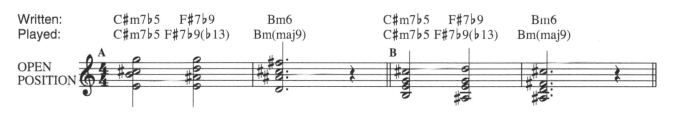

Tonal Center: B Minor

Written: C#m7♭5   F#7♭9   Bm6   C#m7♭5   F#7♭9   Bm6
Played: C#m7♭5   F#7♭9(♭13)   Bm(maj9)   C#m7♭5   F#7♭9(♭13)   Bm(maj9)

OPEN POSITION

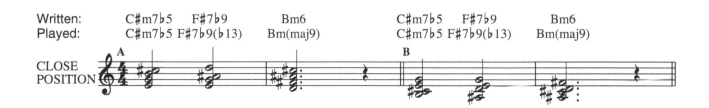

Written: C#m7♭5   F#7♭9   Bm6   C#m7♭5   F#7♭9   Bm6
Played: C#m7♭5   F#7♭9(♭13)   Bm(maj9)   C#m7♭5   F#7♭9(♭13)   Bm(maj9)

CLOSE POSITION

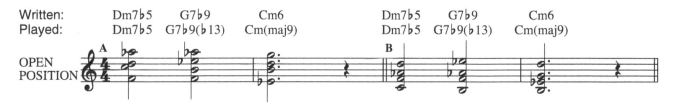

Tonal Center: C Minor

Written: Dm7♭5   G7♭9   Cm6   Dm7♭5   G7♭9   Cm6
Played: Dm7♭5   G7♭9(♭13)   Cm(maj9)   Dm7♭5   G7♭9(♭13)   Cm(maj9)

OPEN POSITION

Written: Dm7♭5   G7♭9   Cm6   Dm7♭5   G7♭9   Cm6
Played: Dm7♭5   G7♭9(♭13)   Cm(maj9)   Dm7♭5   G7♭9(♭13)   Cm(maj9)

CLOSE POSITION

Tonal Center: F♯ Minor

Written: G♯m7♭5   C♯7♭9   F♯m6   G♯m7♭5   C♯7♭9   F♯m6
Played: G♯m7♭5 C♯7♭9(♭13) F♯m(maj9)   G♯m7♭5 C♯7♭9(♭13) F♯m(maj9)

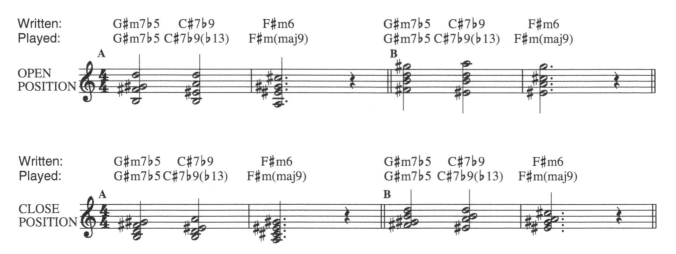

Written: G♯m7♭5   C♯7♭9   F♯m6   G♯m7♭5   C♯7♭9   F♯m6
Played: G♯m7♭5 C♯7♭9(♭13) F♯m(maj9)   G♯m7♭5 C♯7♭9(♭13) F♯m(maj9)

Tonal Center: F Minor

Written: Gm7♭5   C7♭9   Fm6   Gm7♭5   C7♭9   Fm6
Played: Gm7♭5 C7♭9(♭13) Fm(maj9)   Gm7♭5 C7♭9(♭13) Fm(maj9)

Written: Gm7♭5   C7♭9   Fm6   Gm7♭5   C7♭9   Fm6
Played: Gm9♭5 C7♭9(♭13) Fm(maj9)   Gm9♭5 C7♭9(♭13) Fm(maj9)

Tonal Center: C♯ Minor

Written: D♯m7♭5   G♯7♭9   C♯m6   D♯m7♭5   G♯7♭9   C♯m6
Played: D♯m7♭5 G♯7♭9(♭13) C♯m(maj9)   D♯m7♭5 G♯7♭9(♭13) C♯m(maj9)

Written: D♯m7♭5   G♯7♭9   C♯m6   D♯m7♭5   G♯7♭9   C♯m6
Played: D♯m7♭5 G♯7♭9(♭13) C♯m(maj9)   D♯m7♭5 G♯7♭9(♭13) C♯m(maj9)

Tonal Center: B♭ Minor

Written:	Cm7♭5	F7♭9	B♭m6		Cm7♭5	F7♭9	B♭m6
Played:	Cm7♭5	F7♭9(♭13)	B♭m(maj9)		Cm7♭5	F7♭9(♭13)	B♭m(maj9)

OPEN POSITION

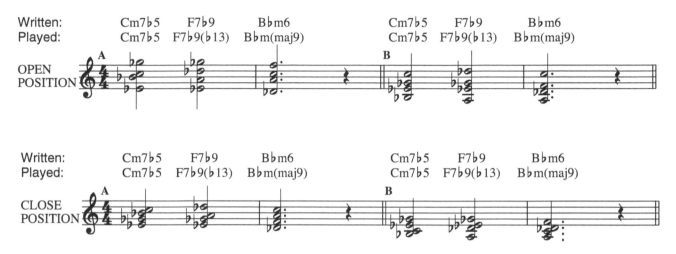

Written:	Cm7♭5	F7♭9	B♭m6		Cm7♭5	F7♭9	B♭m6
Played:	Cm7♭5	F7♭9(♭13)	B♭m(maj9)		Cm7♭5	F7♭9(♭13)	B♭m(maj9)

CLOSE POSITION

Tonal Center: G♯ Minor

Written:	A♯m7♭5	D♯7♭9	G♯m6		A♯m7♭5	D♯7♭9	G♯m6
Played:	A♯m7♭5	D♯7♭9(♭13)	G♯m(maj9)		A♯m7♭5	D♯7♭9(♭13)	G♯m(maj9)

OPEN POSITION

Written:	A♯m7♭5	D♯7♭9	G♯m6		A♯m7♭5	D♯7♭9	G♯m6
Played:	A♯m7♭5	D♯7♭9(♭13)	G♯m(maj9)		A♯m7♭5	D♯7♭9(♭13)	G♯m(maj9)

CLOSE POSITION

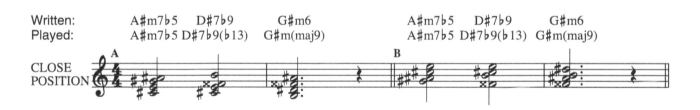

Tonal Center: E♭ Minor

Written:	Fm7♭5	B♭7♭9	E♭m6		Fm7♭5	B♭7♭9	E♭m6
Played:	Fm7♭5	B♭7♭9(♭13)	E♭m(maj9)		Fm7♭5	B♭7♭9(♭13)	E♭m(maj9)

OPEN POSITION

Written:	Fm7♭5	B♭7♭9	E♭m6		Fm7♭5	B♭7♭9	E♭m6
Played:	Fm7♭5	B♭7♭9(♭13)	E♭m(maj9)		Fm7♭5	B♭7♭9(♭13)	E♭m(maj9)

CLOSE POSITION

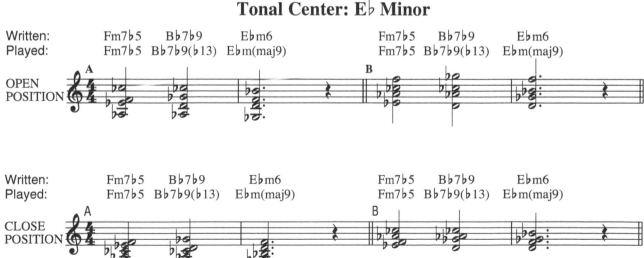

Tonal Center: D♯ Minor

Written: E♯m7♭5   A♯7♭9   D♯m6   E♯m7♭5   A♯7♭9   D♯m6
Played: E♯m7♭5 A♯7♭9(♭13) D♯m(maj9)   E♯m7♭5 A♯7♭9(♭13) D♯m(maj9)

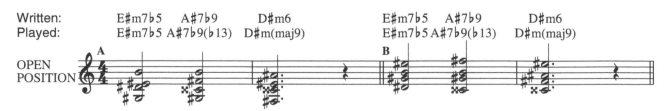

Written: E♯m7♭5   A♯7♭9   D♯m6   E♯m7♭5   A♯7♭9   D♯m6
Played: E♯m7♭5 A♯7♭9(♭13) D♯m(maj9)   E♯m7♭5 A♯7♭9(♭13) D♯m(maj9)

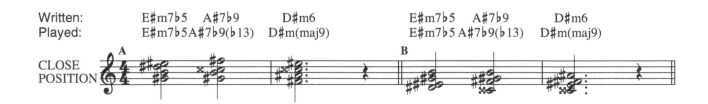

Tonal Center: A♭ Minor

Written: B♭m7♭5   E♭7♭9   A♭m6   B♭m7♭5   E♭7♭9   A♭m6
Played: B♭m7♭5 E♭7♭9(♭13) A♭m(maj9)   B♭m7♭5 E♭7♭9(♭13) A♭m(maj9)

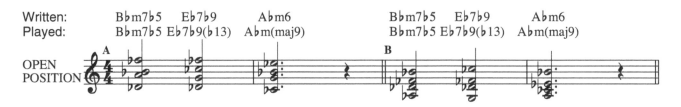

Written: B♭m7♭5   E♭7♭9   A♭m6   B♭m7♭5   E♭7♭9   A♭m6
Played: B♭m7♭5 E♭7♭9(♭13) A♭m(maj9)   B♭m7♭5 E♭7♭9(♭13) A♭m(maj9)

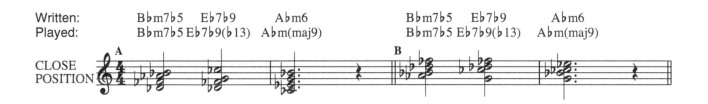

Tonal Center: A♯ Minor

Written: B♯m7♭5   E♯7♭9   A♯m6   B♯m7♭5   E♯7♭9   A♯m6
Played: B♯m7♭5 E♯7♭9(♭13) A♯m(maj9)   B♯m7♭5 E♯7♭9(♭13) A♯m(maj9)

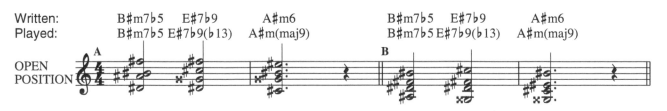

Written: B♯m7♭5   E♯7♭9   A♯m6   B♯m7♭5   E♯7♭9   A♯m6
Played: B♯m7♭5 E♯7♭9(♭13) A♯m(maj9)   B♯m7♭5 E♯7♭9(♭13) A♯m(maj9)

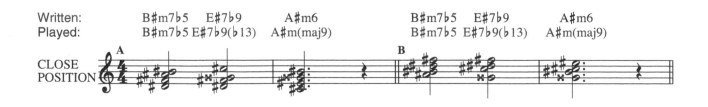

STANDARD CHORD PROGRESSIONS

The following pages contain charts with chord progressions typical of jazz standards. Each chart features comping patterns for vibes using extensions, alterations and rhythmic variations as discussed in the previous chapters.

Each chart is featured in two audio versions. The first features vibes, drums and bass, with the vibes playing the written comping part. The second version features drums and bass only, for use as a play-along track. Once you can comp as written in the chart, feel free to apply your own voicings and rhythmic variations to the chord progressions.

BALLAD

Track ◆1 with vibes
Track ◆2 play-along

MEDIUM SWING

Track ❸ with vibes

Track ❹ play-along

FAST SWING

Track ◆ **with vibes**
Track ◆ **play-along**

34

JAZZ WALTZ

Track ◆⑦ **with vibes**
Track ◆⑧ **play-along**

BOSSA-NOVA

Track 9 with vibes
Track 10 play-along

SAMBA

Track ⑪ with vibes
Track ⑫ play-along